EARTH ALERT!

Transport

Andrew and Amanda Church

WAYLAND   WWF

Produced in Association with WWF UK

Earth Alert!

Coasts
Energy
Farming

Settlements
Transport
Rivers

Cover: Air traffic controllers look out over a busy airport.
Title page: A motorway junction.
Contents page: A bicycle park in China.

First published in 1998 by Wayland Publishers Limited
61 Western Road, Hove
East Sussex, BN3 1JD, England
© Copyright Wayland Publishers Limited 1998

All Wayland books encourage children to read and help them improve their literacy.

✓ The contents page, page numbers, headings and index help locate specific pieces of information.

✓ The glossary reinforces alphabetic knowledge and extends vocabulary.

✓ The further information section suggests other books dealing with the same subject.

WWF UK is a registered charity no. 201707
WWF UK, Panda House, Weyside Park, Godalming,
Surrey GU7 1XR

British Library Cataloguing in Publication Data
Church, Andrew
    Transport. – (Earth alert)
    1. Transportation – Juvenile literature 2. Transportation –
    Environmental aspects – Juvenile literature
    I. Title II. Church, Amanda
    388

ISBN 0 7502 2260 3

Designed by Open Book
Printed and bound in Italy by EuroGrafica.

This book was prepared for
Wayland Publishers Ltd by
Margot Richardson,
23 Hanover Terrace, Brighton, E Sussex, BN2 2SN

Picture acknowledgements
Axiom Photographic Agency (Steve Benbow) 23, (Steve Benbow) 25, (Jim Holmes) 26; James Davis Travel Photography 20; Ecoscene (Melanie Peters) 8, 13, (John Farmar) 28; Eye Ubiquitous (Julia Bayne) 7; (J.C. Pasieka) 21; Foster and Partners 29 both; Impact Photos (Charles Coates) 4, (Christophe Bluntzer) 6, (Trevor Morgan) 12, (Alain Evrard) 24; Tony Stone Images (Paul Chesley) cover, (Baron Wolman) 1, (Don Smetzer) 10, (Richard Brown) 11, (David Woodfall) 14, (Will & Deni McIntyre) 15, (George Hunter) 22; Wayland Picture Library (Julia Waterlow) 3, 5, 16, 18, (A. Blackburn) 19.

Artwork by Peter Bull Art Studio.

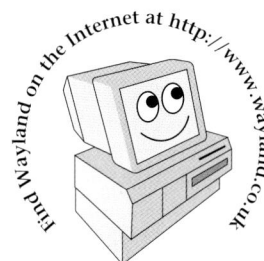

Find Wayland on the Internet at http://www.wayland.co.uk

Contents

Moving Around

A father carries his baby in a sling to do the shopping. The baby sleeps and is content. What neither of them realise is that they are using probably one of the first transport vehicles invented by humans. For early humans, walking was the only way to get around. Nowadays, there are hundreds of different types of transport that move people and goods around the world, ranging from bicycles to aeroplanes and canoes to tankers.

All forms of transport have one thing in common: they use energy to make things move. Walking uses our body's energy that comes from food. A car uses petrol as a source of energy.

Some sources of energy use up natural resources, such as oil, that will eventually run out. Other types of energy will last for ever. Wind power moves sailing ships and power from the sun may drive cars in the future. Wind and the sun are sources of energy that will not run out.

A busy street in India is filled with many different types of transport.

All forms of transport can have a bad effect on our environment, whatever the energy source. For example, we all know that cars create air pollution. Although walking has very little impact, too many hikers in one place can destroy footpaths and damage areas of natural beauty.

We need to use transport for many reasons, such as for going to school, holidays, shopping, business and going to work.

Moving around is essential to our lives, but in future we will have to find forms of transport that cause less harm to the environment. We may also have to move around less.

The skateboard above, roller blades, ice skates, skis and surfboards are all types of transport.

The development of transport

Until 200 years ago, the main forms of transport and sources of energy were:

- Walking using human energy.
- Wind-powered sailing ships on the sea.
- Carts and carriages using energy from horses.

In the nineteenth and twentieth centuries a range of inventions changed transport for ever.

1769–1813	Steam boats and trains developed.
1783	Air transport began with the first hot-air balloon.
1880s	Internal combustion engine used in first motorized vehicles.
1900–10	First aeroplanes.
1961	Yuri Gagarin first person to travel in space.

Did you jump in the car to get to school today? Could you have walked instead? Walking to school would have used less energy and caused less harm to the environment.

Local Journeys Using Body Energy

The most common journeys people make are in their local area, near to where they live. These journeys are quite short. They might be trips to school, work, the shops or to see friends and relatives. Many of these journeys can be done by walking or cycling using energy made by our bodies. The food we eat is digested and our blood and muscles turn it into energy that allows us to move.

Animals as transport

In a similar way, the body energy of animals can be used to transport people and goods. In many farming areas of the world, animals such as horses, oxen, bullocks, yaks and even dogs are used to pull heavy loads.

Horse-drawn carts in Romania. Animals are a slow form of transport.

Bicycles

Bicycles are a good way to use body energy for transport. The pedals and chain transfer energy from people's legs to the wheels. Bicycles allow us to travel further and faster than we could if we walked using the same amount of energy.

There are about 850 million bicycles in the world. Bicycles are not harmful to the environment as they cause little or no pollution. They are good for you as well: cycling is an excellent form of exercise.

However, many people avoid using bicycles because they feel roads are too dangerous. Some cities are trying to make it easier and safer for people to cycle. In Odense, in Denmark, special bike-only routes have made cycling safer, and six out of ten children cycle to school.

Bike-only routes are a safe and easy way for moving around a local area.

Finding what we need locally

Using local shops is less harmful to our environment than travelling to shops some distance away. By travelling shorter distances we use less energy and create less pollution.

In poorer countries, outside big cities, people often have no choice. They cannot afford forms of transport other than walking, so they walk to buy or collect what they need. For example, in many developing countries, people spend over three hours each day collecting the wood that is their only source of fuel.

Using energy

Different forms of transport use up different amounts of energy. Energy use is measured in megajoules. This table shows you how much energy different types of transport use when travelling round a town.

TYPE OF TRANSPORT	MEGAJOULES OF ENERGY PER PERSON PER KM
Large car	4.23
Motorbike	2.67
Small car	2.42
Bus (half full)	0.62
Train (two-thirds full)	0.56
Walking	0.25
Cycling	0.06

In richer countries, most of us have a choice as to how we travel around our local area. We can walk, cycle, take a bus or drive. Too often we use a car to make a short journey without even thinking of other ways of travelling. In the UK for example, 70 per cent of car journeys are under 8 km, a distance that many people could cycle.

In richer countries, many people use their cars all the time, even when there are other forms of transport.

The DEPO transport system

A new form of public transport is being developed in Amsterdam, the capital city of the Netherlands.

The idea for the 'White Bike System' was first used in Amsterdam in the 1960s. Large numbers of bicycles were painted white to make them look different from private bicycles. If someone needed to go somewhere they used a white bicycle then left it on the street at their destination for another person to use. However, eventually all the bicycles disappeared, and the system did not work any more.

Now this idea has been updated using a computer system to control hiring bicycles around the city. The person who wants hire the bike uses a special 'smart' card, (like a credit card) to book the trip, pay and reserve a parking space at his or her destination. The computer also prints out a route of where the person wants to go.

The DEPO system is still being developed, so it cannot be used in many places yet. However, it aims to improve public transport and make it easier for people to move around the city.

People using a computer to hire 'white bikes' in Amsterdam.

Food and transport

In cities all over the world, many people drive to out-of-town shopping centres to buy food rather than going to their nearest shops. Often the food they buy has travelled a long way to get to these shops. Next time you buy an apple find out where it has come from. It might have been carried from New Zealand or Canada by plane or boat.

In the USA, many cities now have a farmers' market. The food on sale is grown in the local area and has been transported only a short distance. This uses less energy and so causes less pollution.

Transport for all

Walking and cycling are easier for some people than others. In Europe, for example, one in ten people have difficulty walking up steps. These are mainly older people or some people who are disabled. Many of these people can only walk if pavements do not have too many obstacles, such as cracks and steps. Too many steps and rough pavements are also difficult for very young children, and for parents pushing children in prams or buggies.

Streets and pavements should be designed so they can be used by everyone. This must include people who have problems walking and people who are disabled.

Activity

School transport survey

Working in a group draw up a list of questions to ask the whole class. You are trying to find out:

- How they travel to and from school.
- How long their journey takes.
- How far they travel.

Make sure you use words that are clear and will obtain the information you want. Discuss with the teacher the lists each group has made and agree a set of questions that should be completed by the whole class.

Ask each pupil to complete the survey at home. They may need some help with how far they travel and how long it takes.

In the USA, many children can take a special school bus to get to school.

Use this information to create pictorial graphs of the journey to school of pupils in the class.

Work out roughly how much energy each pupil uses to get to school using the fact box on page 8. Write down ways you think pupils could change how they travel to school so that they use less energy.

Journeys Using Energy from the Environment

Methods of transport such as buses, trains and trams allow people to travel more quickly around local areas. The environment provides the energy for these vehicles. The energy sources include oil and coal, which are burnt, and energy in the form of electricity.

Cars and buses

Cars and buses use petrol or diesel for energy, which comes from oil. Burning oil causes serious pollution.

Trains and trams

Different types of trains may be used for local journeys. In some countries, older trains run on diesel fuel or coal. Buses, trains and trams are known as public transport, because anyone can travel on them.

This tram in Melbourne, Australia, runs on electricity from overhead wires.

The impact of an electric train or tram on the environment will depend on how the electricity has been made. If it comes from a power station making electricity by burning coal, oil or gas this will create pollution and use up fuel. If the power station uses wind or water as the source of energy then it creates far less pollution and does not use up fuels that cannot be replaced.

In many countries people are using cars even when buses, trains or trams are available.

Why do people prefer to drive?

Cars allow people to make a lot of short journeys one after another. Cars take people right to where they want to go. In bad weather a car provides shelter. For disabled people, cars may be the only way they can travel easily. Many people feel safer from crime travelling by car compared to travelling by public transport. In some areas, especially remote countryside, people use cars because there are not enough buses and trains.

The number of cars in the world is set to increase from about 600 million now to 750 million by 2005. Many people who do not own a car would like to buy one.

Pollution from cars

Two of the gases from car exhaust are nitrogen oxide and hydrocarbons.

On sunny days they mix with sunlight to form smog which makes it hard for some people to breathe.

Nitrogen oxide mixes with water in the clouds to make acid rain which damages buildings and harms plants and wildlife.

The problems caused by cars

Cars are one of the biggest causes of air pollution, which can harm people's health.

They also produce carbon dioxide, which is one of the 'greenhouse gases'. These gases form a layer around the Earth and trap heat near its surface. Without this layer of gases, the Earth would be very cold and could not support life.

The gases in car exhausts are bad for people's health and cause air pollution.

However, more and more of these gases are being released into the atmosphere. This is making the Earth warmer, and it may change climates all over the world. This could have serious effects for everyone. Food production would be affected, many countries would be flooded, serious diseases may spread and some plants and animals would die out.

In some countries people are so worried about air pollution from cars that new laws have been passed. Car companies are being forced to make cars with very few polluting gases in their exhaust.

People imagine the car to be the quickest form of transport for short journeys, but in cities the roads are often so clogged by traffic that journeys take longer than they should. Cars have made some roads very busy, especially in the rush hour at the beginning and end of a working day.

Traffic jams make road travel slower. They also increase the pollution caused by cars.

Activity

Investigate traffic flow

Working in small groups, choose a busy road near your school to investigate traffic. Count how many cars, lorries, vans and bicycles go by in a 15-minute period. Make a table to present this information. Back in the classroom draw a graph to display the results.

How many people are there in each vehicle during the same 15-minute period? Work out a way of displaying this information. Could people share cars? How would this change the number of cars on the road?

What is the most common vehicle? Do most cars have a driver and no passengers? Consider the alternative forms of transport in your area. Could the road be made safer for pedestrians and bicycles?

All these problems caused by the car effect everyone in a country. This is unfair on people who do not have a car. They get all the problems of cars without having the benefits of owning one.

What can we use instead of the car?

Moving a large number of people by bus or train uses much less energy than if the same number of people all used cars. Using public transport, such as buses, trams or trains is better for the environment than using cars. Public transport reduces the number of cars on the roads.

A train in Argentina. Trains are an efficient way of moving a large number of people.

To encourage people to use public transport it must be safe, not too expensive, stop near people's homes, arrive on time and be pleasant to use. The problem is that good public transport costs money, but so does building roads for cars and cleaning up their pollution.

Using cars

Mark and Beth Malallieu live with their four children in Luray, Virginia, a small town about two and a half hours from Washington DC, the capital of the USA.

Mark works as a manager in a factory. To get to work he has to drive 45 km. He uses the family's small car. He says there is no alternative to using a car: 'There are no local buses and I don't even know where the nearest railway station is.'

Beth is a registered nurse at the local hospital. Although her journey is only 1.6 km, she drives the family's other car, a six-seater. 'I could cycle to work but I have to drop Thomas, who is three, off at his child minder first. To be honest, I just wouldn't feel safe coming home on a bike late at night. A car is much more convenient.' The other three children get themselves to school by walking five minutes down the road.

Mark explained that there is no public transport around their local area. 'There are no local buses and the nearest Greyhound coach station is 32 km away. Everyone we know around here has a car, and most people have two.'

There is no public transport where the Malallieus live, so they use their cars all the time.

Long-distance Transport

Many of the journeys that transport people and goods outside their local area are made for business reasons. Some journeys are made by car, but over long distances trains and aeroplanes can be much quicker.

Some companies are trying to reduce the time their staff spend travelling by using video links for meetings. That way people in different places – even on other sides of the world – can see each other talking without travelling.

Freight

Goods are moved around a country by lorry, train, aeroplane or boat. The means of transport depends on the cost, the speed and the size of the load.

- Boats on big rivers, such as the Mississippi, in the USA, can move heavy loads cheaply but slowly.
- Train and lorry transport is quicker but is often more expensive. Many businesses prefer to use lorries because goods can go directly to their destination which saves time and money.
- Aeroplanes are an expensive way to transport goods and are mostly used to move something in a hurry that is valuable and does not weigh very much.

Ships on the River Rhine in Germany. Around the world, many rivers are major transport routes.

Environmental impact

For moving goods, boats tend to cause least damage to the environment since they use the smallest amount of energy for each tonne of goods.

Lorries probably do the most environmental harm because they create pollution from their exhausts, damage roads and shake buildings. Lorries use a lot more energy for each tonne of goods compared to a train or a boat, because each lorry only carries a small load.

Planes move many people quickly but jet engine fuel creates harmful gases.

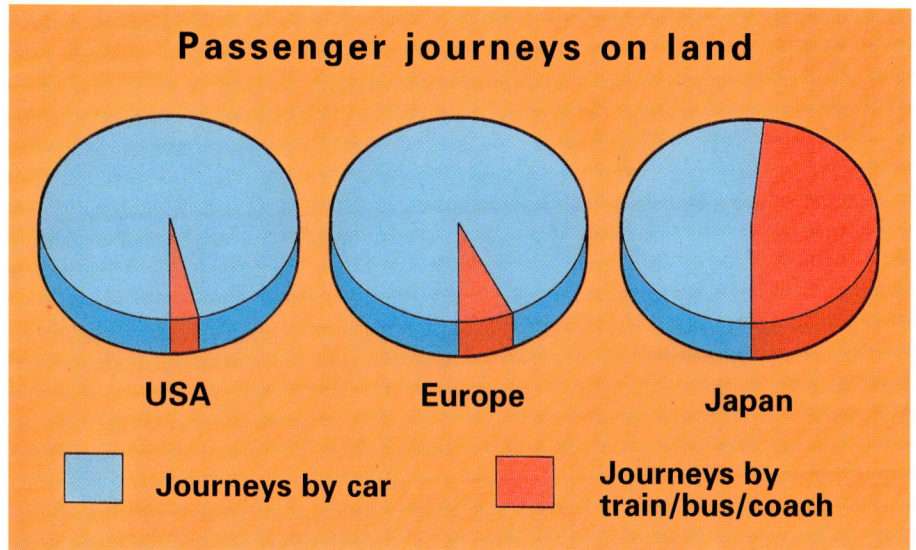

Passenger journeys on land

USA   Europe   Japan

Journeys by car   Journeys by train/bus/coach

Activity

Measuring congestion

People and goods need to get to their destination on time. If roads or routes are crowded, transport will be slowed down.

Each transport route has a capacity. This is the amount of vehicles it can carry safely and at a reasonable speed. Congestion occurs when there are more vehicles than the route can carry.

You can do this exercise in the school hall or a large room. You will need a stopwatch, two chairs and the whole class.

1 Put the chairs about 2 m apart and line up the class in pairs.
2 The pairs then move between the chairs as quickly as possible without bumping into each other. Time how long it takes.
3 Then try it in groups of threes and fours. The capacity of the gap between the chairs is reached when the number of children trying to move through at the same time start bumping into each other and congestion occurs. What is the capacity of the gap?
4 Repeat the experiment with a 1 m or a 3 m gap.

Imagine the gap between the chairs is a door and your class is having to go through it in an emergency. Have a discussion about the safest way to leave your classroom in an emergency.

A crowded street in Delhi, India. Congestion happens where there are too many people or vehicles for the space available.

In some countries travel beyond the local area is difficult. Their governments do not have much money, so roads and railways are not very good, or do not exist at all. In these countries, river and air transport is often the only reliable way to travel long distances.

CASE STUDY

Transport in Gabon

Jean Ivombo lives with his wife Eugenie and their three children in Gamba, a small town in Gabon, West Africa. He works for Shell Gabon at an oil terminal on the coast.

For their annual holiday, Jean and his family visit Eugenie's parents in the small village of Ndende, deep in the rain forest. It is possible to take a bush taxi but it takes 10 hours to cover the 380 km as the roads are often washed away by tropical storms, and are very bumpy. Even though it is much more expensive, Jean chooses to fly and then cover the last section of the journey by taxi.

The government in Gabon would like to build better roads, but is worried that this will open up the rain forest areas too much. People may move in and cut down the trees to make land for farming.

Improving road transport would make life easier for people in Gabon, but the rain forest would be damaged in the process. Rain forests are very important because they contain many rare species of plants and animals. They also help to control the earth's climate.

Jean Ivombo and his family like to travel to the rain forest.

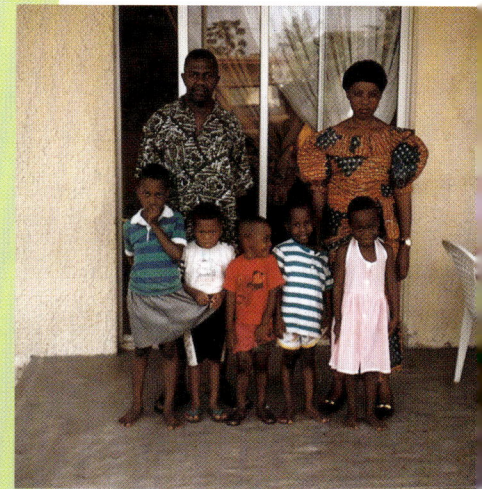

Making new roads through forest land destroys the natural landscape.

International Travel

Goods and ships

Goods sent between countries separated by sea are usually moved by ship. Goods on a ship are called cargo. They are often packed into containers, which are huge metal boxes that stack on top of each other. Supertankers, which carry oil, are the largest forms of transport in the world. Some are 450 m long.

International travel is too expensive for most people in the world, but more tourists visit other countries for their holiday than ever before.

Transport and holidays

Planes, cars and fast trains have allowed many people to travel much further on holiday than they used to 30 years ago. For example, in 1985 about 3 million people from Europe visited the United States. Now it is about 9 million people a year and nearly all of them travel by plane.

Tourism can have good and bad effects on the places people visit.

The benefits of tourism

Tourism brings money to a country and creates jobs for the people who live there. New shops and roads built for tourists may be useful for local people. Travelling abroad allows people from different countries to meet and perhaps understand each other better.

The problems of tourism

Tourism can destroy the places people travel to see. For example, ancient Roman and Greek buildings in Europe have been damaged by huge numbers of people walking in them.

Tourists can also harm the environment and animal wildlife. In the Caribbean, extra waste caused by tourism has poisoned mangrove swamps and divers have damaged coral reefs.

In poor countries, valuable land, food, water and fuel may be used for tourists instead of local people. In places where few people have ever visited, tourism can change the way of life. Remote tribes of people in South America and Asia have been infected by diseases they had never known before tourists brought them into the area.

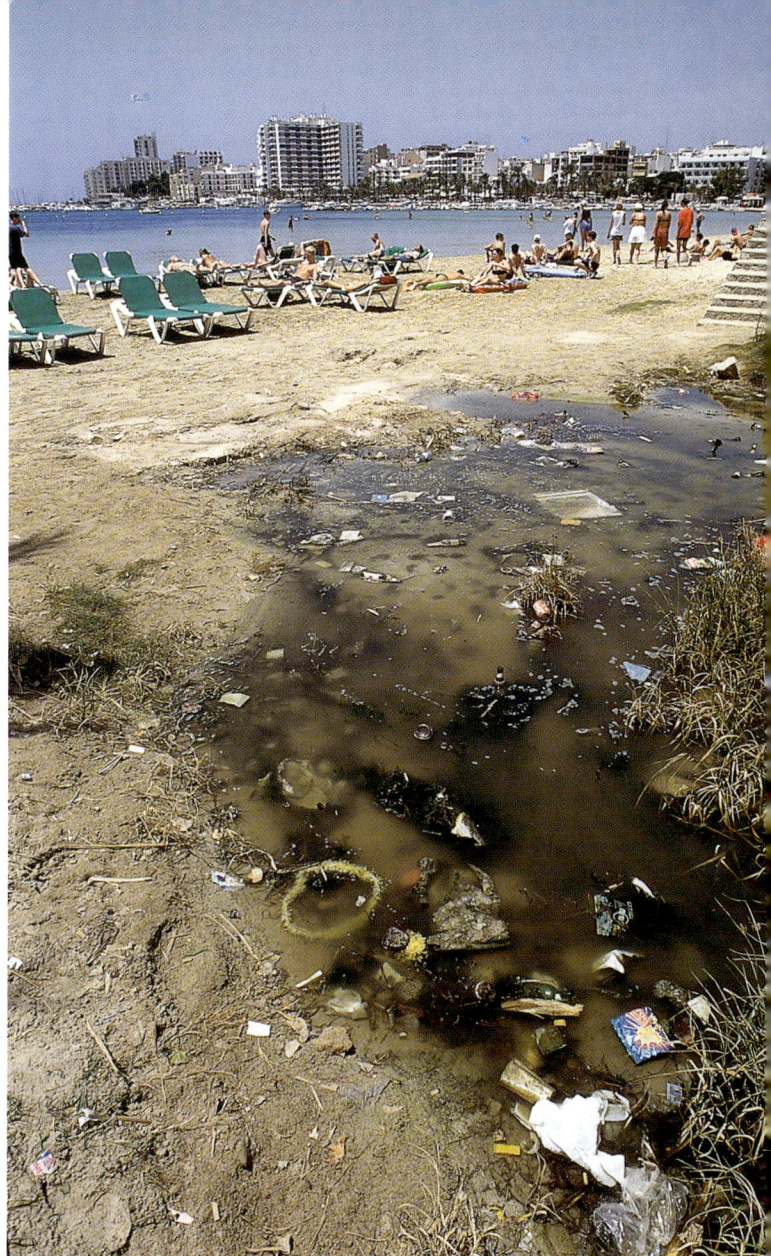

Popular holiday areas such as Florida and Spain (above) have been spoilt by too many large hotels and pollution.

Tourism in the Mediterranean

- Each year, over 160 million people visit the coastal areas and islands of the Mediterranean Sea.
- Three-quarters of the sand dunes between Gibraltar in Spain and Sicily in Italy have disappeared because of new buildings.
- Hotel building in part of Turkey was stopped to save a type of turtle, called the loggerhead turtle. The building was destroying the turtles' habitat. Now the turtles attract an extra 5,000 tourists a year, creating other environmental problems.

Tourism in Bali

Bali is one of the smallest islands in Indonesia. It lies 8 degrees south of the equator and has a pleasant, warm climate. The island has a population of 3.5 million people. The Balinese people follow the Hindu religion and have many colourful ceremonies and festivals. Painting, dancing, music, puppet-making and kite flying are popular pastimes.

As a result of cheap air travel, many hotels have been built in Bali.

The first tourists came to Bali in the 1920s, travelling by ship. European people opened a few hotels in the 1950s and 1960s. When the first beach hotel was opened at Sanur, in 1966, Balinese people came from all over the island to see the running water, electricity and elevators.

The 1970s brought cheap international air travel, and large numbers of people started to come to Bali. Now more than 350,000 people visit every year, flying in from Europe, the USA and Australia.

New roads and highways have been built; hotels, shops, restaurants and nightclubs have opened, night markets are held and roads in tourist areas are full of cars and motorbikes. While many Balinese people have made money and improved their standard of living, parts of Bali have changed forever as a result of cheap international air travel.

Tourists visiting another country can try to reduce the harmful effects of tourism, such as pollution. They choose to visit places where their visit will not damage the environment or change other people's way of life.

A group of tourists on the Galapagos Islands, South America. They are learning about the islands' unique animals and plants.

Activity

Being a good tourist

Imagine some schoolchildren are going to visit your local area. They come from another country where the way of life is different. They have written to you wanting to know how to be a good tourist in a your area. They want to know:

- The best places to visit in your local area.
- How they should travel around your local area.
- How they should behave in public places and shops.
- What to do if they bump into someone or get in their way.
- How they should behave in cafés and restaurants.

Make a postcard to send them. Divide the front into four quarters and in each quarter draw a picture of one of the places you think they should visit. Write on the back giving answers to their questions.

Transport in the Future

People move around for many reasons, from shopping near their homes to going on holiday on the other side of the world.

Using cars less

The most common form of transport around the world is the car. Car transport is a particular problem because it creates pollution and each car does not move very many people. We need to encourage people to use cars less. Some organizations have suggested that governments should:

- Spend more on buses, trains and trams. This would make public transport a good alternative to cars, especially for long trips.
- Encourage people who drive to work to share cars.
- Build safe routes to school so children can walk and cycle.
- Stop companies building out-of-town shopping centres, because most people have to drive to them.
- Make driving more expensive by putting up prices of petrol and car-parks.
- Make more city areas car free, so they are pleasant for pedestrians and cyclists.

It is difficult for children to walk to school if they do not have safe footpaths.

Less damage to the environment

The car is not the only problem. All transport uses energy and has some impact on the environment.

To reduce environmental damage we need to change how we live and we must move around less. We could do this by:

- Working from home, using computers, phone modems and faxes. In the USA, nearly 4 million people now work from home.
- Shopping from home, ordering goods by computer which are then delivered to people's homes.
- Encouraging people to use local shops and to buy food that is grown locally.
- Building new houses near city centres and places where there are jobs, so people do not have to travel so far to where they work.

A covered market in Portugal. Buying food that has been made or grown locally uses less energy.

In the future there will be many new forms of transport, on land, on the sea, and in the air.

Some amazing transport inventions will allow the richer people in the world to travel further and faster using less energy and making less pollution. New types of supersonic airplanes that will be quieter, bigger and quicker than Concorde are being planned. Cars that use energy from the sun have already been made, and they may be developed further for countries that have plenty of sun.

But not everyone in the world will benefit from these changes. We also need to develop transport ideas that poorer people can use to make their lives easier and more pleasant.

A few solar-powered cars have been built by big car companies. This car attracts interest in a street in Australia.

Activity

Pedestrianization

Parliament Square in London as it is now, with traffic driving through it.

This exercise examines the advantages and problems of the different ways of moving around a small area. A pedestrianized road is one that is closed to cars and only pedestrians, bikes and emergency vehicles are allowed into the area.

Government officials in London are planning to pedestrianize parts of Trafalgar Square and Parliament Square. They contain some of the best known tourist sites in the world, such as Nelson's Column, Westminster Abbey and the Houses of Parliament. The area is very busy with tourists, office workers, cars and buses.

Act out the following parts and discuss the benefits and problems of changing the squares.

- A tourist visiting Trafalgar Square.
- Someone who lives in a nearby street that is to be used by more cars and buses.
- A van driver delivering to offices.
- A local café owner.
- A person in a wheelchair visiting Westminster Abbey.
- An official who wants to reduce car pollution.

After the role play, talk about all the different ideas and feelings. Would it be a good idea to change the area?

This is how Parliament Square might look after pedestrianization.

29

Glossary

Acid rain Rain containing pollution from vehicles and industry.

Atmosphere The gases surrounding the earth.

Congestion Too many vehicles or people for the space available, causing it to clog up.

Destination The place to which someone or something is travelling.

Disabled Being unable to walk or move well.

Emergency vehicles Fire, police, ambulance and rescue vehicles.

Environment Everything, both living and non-living, that surrounds and affects a living thing.

Freight Goods to be transported.

Fuel Something that can be burnt to give energy.

Generate Make or produce electricity, light or heat.

Internal combustion engine An engine which burns fuel inside a cylinder.

International Between two different countries.

Local Near to a particular area.

Mangrove swamps Large numbers of mangrove trees growing in wet muddy areas on the edges of rivers and coasts.

Natural resources Anything from the earth or its atmosphere that is useful, such as oil, wood or wind.

Pedestrian A person who travels on foot.

Pedestrianize Make a street or an area for pedestrians only.

Pollution Damage to air, water or land by harmful materials.

Public transport A form of transport that can be used by everybody.

Rush hour The periods of the day when large numbers of people travel to and from work.

Smog A harmful mixture of smoke, moisture and gases that forms in the air over towns.

Source of energy Where the power to make something move or work comes from.

Technology The use of science to make advances in industry or business.

Tourist A person who travels for pleasure.

Vehicle Something that carries and moves people or goods, on land or in space.

Resources

Topic Web — TRANSPORT

MUSIC
- Rhythms/sounds of transport forms
- Songs about journeys and travelling

GEOGRAPHY
- Comparing and grouping different forms of transport
- Scale of journeys
- Map work
- Environmental, economic and social effects
- Links between places

HISTORY
- Changing forms of transport
- Role of transport in social/economic development

ART & CRAFT
- Drawing street scenes and transport
- Postcards and travel posters

DESIGN AND TECHNOLOGY
- Designing and constructing boats, vehicles and flying machines

MATHS
- Recording, manipulating and analysing data
- Graphs and diagrams

SCIENCE
- Sources and uses of transport energy
- Human body and movement
- Motion, capacity and congestion
- Managing experiments

ENGLISH
- Stories and poems about journeys
- Writing about travel and tourism

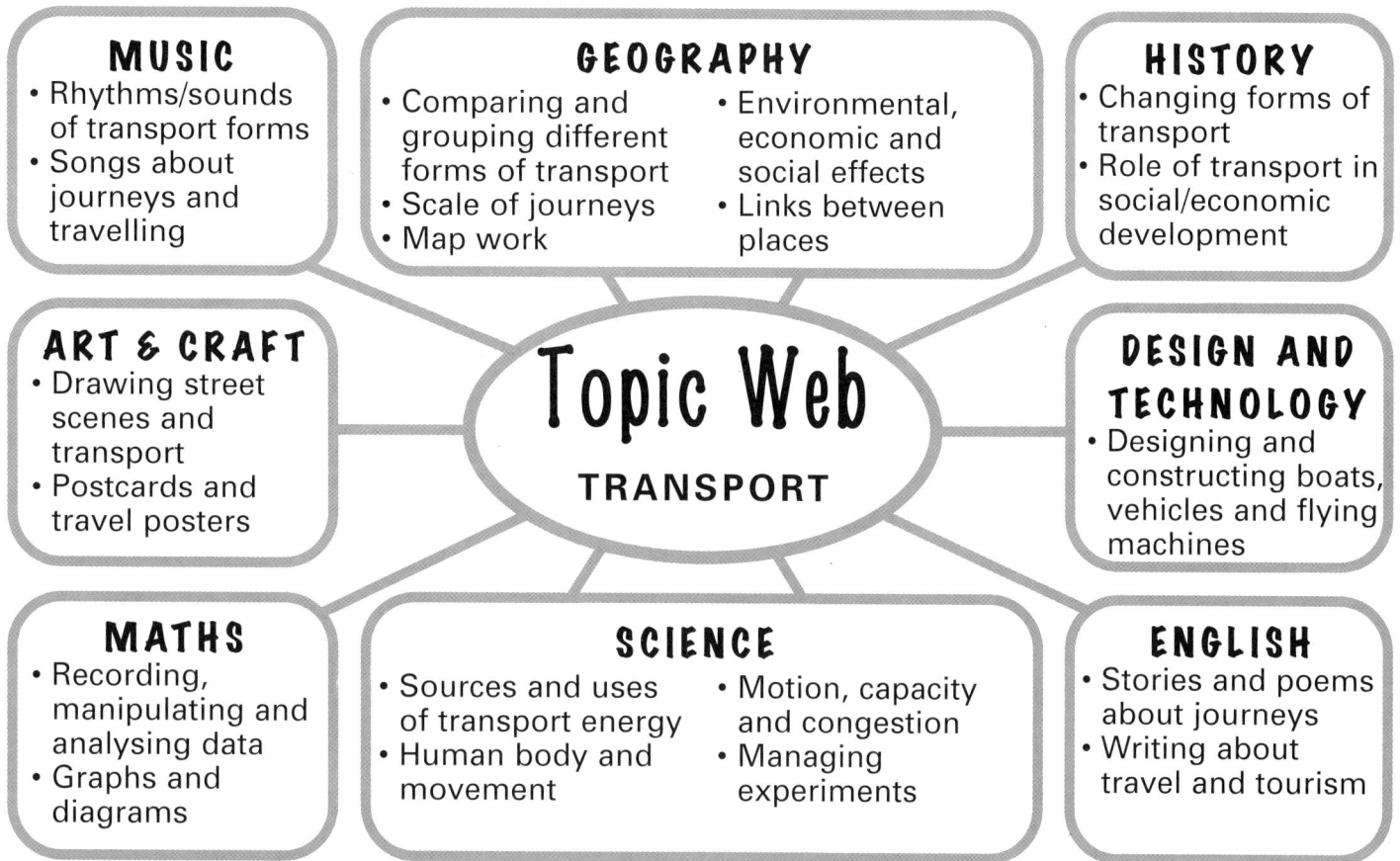

Further information

Books
Design and Make: Wheels and Transport by John Williams, (Wayland, 1997).
History Makers of the Industrial Revolution by Nigel Smith, (Wayland, 1995).
The Great Iron Horse: The Story of Robert Stephenson's Rocket by Margaret Nash, (Macdonald Young Books, 1997).
Make It Work!: Ships and *Make It Work!: Flight* by Andrew Haslam, (Franklin Watts, 1996).
New Technology: Transport on Land and Sea by Nigel Hawkes (Franklin Watts, 1995).
The Unsinkable Titanic by Andrew Donkin, (Macdonald Young Books, 1998).

Multimedia
The Way Things Work 2.0, Dorling Kindersley.

Places to visit

Light rail and trams: London Docklands Light Railway, Sheffield Tramlink, Tyne and Wear Metro, Manchester Metrolink, Blackpool trams.
Major ports: Liverpool, Tilbury, Southampton, Teesside, Dover, the Humber estuary, the Clyde estuary, Bristol at Avonmouth, Port Talbot.
Major airports: Manchester, Leeds, East Midlands, Glasgow, Cardiff, Heathrow, Gatwick, Stanstead, London City Airport, Luton.
Old steam railways: Blaenau Festinniog, North Wales; Pickering, Yorkshire; Bluebell Line, Sussex; Watercress Line, Hampshire; Dart Valley Line; Severn Valley Line; Boat of Garten Line, Scotland.
Museums: London Transport; Beamish Open Air, County Durham; Doxford Air, Cambridgeshire; National Maritime, Greenwich; Maritime Museum, Swansea; Fishing Museum, Aberdeen; Former Royal Yacht Britannia, Leith, Scotland; Railway Museums at York, Swindon and Crewe.

Index